Where Is WITHDRAWN
Area 51?

by Paula K. Manzanero

illustrated by Tim Foley

Penguin Workshop
An Imprint of Penguin Random House

For everyone who wonders what's out there—PM

For Bud, in case the truth actually *is* out there . . .—TF

PENGUIN WORKSHOP
Penguin Young Readers Group
An Imprint of Penguin Random House LLC

Library of Congress Cataloging-in-Publication Data is available.

ISBN 9781524786410 (paperback)   10 9 8 7 6 5 4 3 2 1
ISBN 9781524786427 (library binding)   10 9 8 7 6 5 4 3 2 1

Contents

Where Is Area 51?

On June 14, 1947, a ranch worker named William Brazel found a pile of strange items smack in the middle of an open field near Roswell, New Mexico. It included some wood, foil, and rubber. Where had these things come from? They weren't things that belonged out on the ranch. When Brazel went to town on July 7, he told the local sheriff about

William Brazel

what he'd found, who immediately reported the findings to the US Army Air Force base nearby in Alamogordo. The sheriff thought all of these things probably had come from the army airfield, which was just down the road.

Right away, US government scientists arrived to investigate. They said that the found objects had been pieces of a crashed weather balloon. The Army Air Force had been testing large weather balloons in the area during a powerful storm earlier in the week.

This made sense, but some people were suspicious. Men from the base had arrived so quickly and cleaned the site so well. Were they trying to hide something? If so, what could it be?

On July 8, the *Roswell Daily Record* printed a startling headline that said "RAAF Captures Flying Saucer On Ranch in Roswell Region." (The RAAF was the Roswell Army Air Field.) And the headline, although later corrected, fueled one of the greatest mysteries in US history.

Why would the newspaper print a story that wasn't true? The residents of Roswell began to wonder. Some people—including many who lived nowhere near the town—began telling stories of metal beams and strange objects that had been recovered at Roswell. They believed the first newspaper story was true. They said that the army had removed all evidence of a flying saucer and its alien passengers.

As years passed, many of these people came to believe the "evidence" had been taken to a secret government site deep in the Nevada desert. The site was two states and nearly nine hundred miles away, on the edge of Groom Lake. It was referred to simply by its location on the map: Area 51, one of the most secretive, off-limits places on the planet.

CHAPTER 1
Just a Space on the Map

Area 51 is located in the southern corner of Nevada, in the harsh Mojave Desert of the western United States. There were originally iron and silver mines and small mining communities dotting the flat, dry landscape that includes mesas, salt flats, and dry lake beds of hardened clay.

In 1942, there were only two dirt runways on the property near Groom Lake. The area was used by the US Army for bomb practice. The number fifty-one in Area 51 is believed to refer to the parcel of land as named on the surveyor's map created in the early 1950s.

It was in these types of lonely desert areas of the American southwest that bombing tests could be conducted—including tests of the nuclear weapons used in World War II. The types of nuclear weapons that were being tested were explosive devices that released huge

Hydrogen bomb

amounts of destructive energy. These included the hydrogen bomb and the atomic bomb.

The US bases that developed these weapons included Los Alamos and Alamogordo, both in the state of New Mexico.

The Manhattan Project

During World War II, the United States began developing the atomic bomb. This secret work was known as the Manhattan Project—the name came from the part of New York City where many of the scientists had worked. The team was also in charge of finding ways to spy on German scientists who were trying to create their own atomic bomb. Nuclear physicist J. Robert Oppenheimer was the director of the laboratory that designed the bombs in Los Alamos, New Mexico. The first nuclear device ever exploded was at the nearby Alamogordo range on July 16, 1945. In early August, US atomic bombs were dropped on the Japanese cities of Hiroshima and Nagasaki, killing and injuring more than a hundred thousand people. Japan surrendered a few days later on August 15, 1945, ending the war.

Robert Oppenheimer on left

Because even a small nuclear bomb can devastate an entire city, wide-open and unpopulated spaces were the safest places to test them. The US government also felt that the desert provided enough privacy for these top secret projects.

Area 51 sits just outside America's only atomic bomb range, which was called the Nevada Test Site. From 1951 to 1992, nuclear weapons were exploded aboveground and underground in tunnels and specially drilled shafts.

At first, the site was called "Paradise Ranch" to attract employees. The Central Intelligence Agency (CIA) conducted background checks on anyone wanting to work there.

CIA agents asked each job applicant's friends and neighbors if they thought the person might be a foreign spy. The CIA wanted to be absolutely certain that everyone working at the site could be trusted.

The land around the Nevada Test Site belonged to the Atomic Energy Commission. The US government has always referred to it simply— and mysteriously—as an "operating site," never acknowledging the existence of Area 51 until as late as 1998!

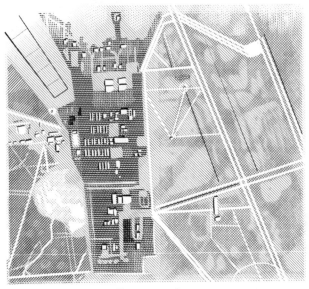
Satellite view of Area 51

Originally only six miles wide and ten miles long, Area 51 came to encompass over four hundred square miles of restricted land and airspace. (*Restricted* means that the area is very tightly controlled.) A large military airfield sits at its center, on the southern edge of Groom Lake. This dry lake bed, about three miles across, has become a US government landing strip for experimental aircraft. These are new types of planes that are developed with the very latest technologies.

CHAPTER 2
Gathering Intelligence

Originally a lead and silver mine, the land inside of Area 51 was acquired by the US Air Force from the Atomic Energy Commission in 1955. It was going to be used for flight testing, mostly by the CIA.

The CIA collects and studies national security information from around the world. This information—called intelligence—is usually top secret and known only to a few CIA agents at a time. The CIA provides these details to the president and some cabinet members so that they can be informed and make the best decisions to keep the United States safe.

At Area 51, besides gathering intelligence, the government was also working to create new metals, plastics, and rubber—as well as new kinds of aircraft—that could not be detected by radar. They wanted planes that could fly unseen by enemy technology. These are known as stealth aircraft. Research for such a sneaky operation was a great fit for the CIA. Their agents were masters of working quietly behind the scenes, away from public view.

Area 51 is well hidden, sitting inside Nevada's high desert within a ring of mountain ranges. And there is another plus: The hard-packed clay of the dry lake bed can support the weight of any aircraft. By 1955, the base had a five-thousand-foot runway, a trailer park where employees lived, three airplane hangars, and a few small buildings.

The security was very tight. There was only one gate into the property. The base was not easy to access. And that's just the way the CIA wanted it.

And because the United States was in the middle of what is known as the Cold War, the CIA wanted to move quickly to test and approve new planes at Area 51.

The Cold War

During the period from about 1947 through 1991, the tension between the United States and the Soviet Union was called the Cold War. (The Soviet Union was a group of national republics controlled by the central government in Russia.) The fighting of World War II was over, and the word *cold* meant that there were no battles being fought.

Harry Truman, US president from 1945 to 1953

The United States and the Soviet Union, which had emerged as the two biggest superpowers in the world, began an intense period of spying and information gathering on each other. The Cold War was a race to have the biggest and best military, weapons, and technology in the world.

Joseph Stalin, Soviet Union leader from 1922 to 1953

At Area 51, the CIA was working hard to outsmart the Soviet Union.

During the Cold War, there was a great fear of Communism in the United States. (The Soviet Union was Communist.) The United States was afraid that if Communism spread to other countries around the world, more nations would become allies of the Soviet Union.

It was a time of great suspicion between the United States and the Soviet Union because the two governments wondered how much each knew about the technological advances of the other's weapons. They both wanted to find out. And they began a long period of surveillance, close and constant observation of people and places.

The United States was opposed to Communism, which doesn't allow democracy. In a democracy, all people have the right, as individuals, to choose their own jobs and achieve whatever level of success is open to them.

Cold War Europe

What Is Communism?

Communists believe a country's government should have control over how people live and work. A Communist society doesn't believe that people should work to make a profit for themselves. The government owns factories and businesses, and the freedom of individuals—such as freedom of speech—is very limited.

The United States also believes in free elections and freedom of the press. It felt that stopping the spread of Communism was the right thing to do.

One of the ways the United States and the Soviet Union collected intelligence on each other was by secretly listening for information about their enemies.

This was exactly the kind of technology that the US government had been developing near Roswell during World War II.

CHAPTER 3
The Roswell Connection

From 1947 to 1949, Alamogordo Army Air Field became the launch site for testing high-altitude balloons that carried microphones. This was an early form of eavesdropping. The US government wanted to develop the technology to listen in on the enemy. The New Mexico–based project, known as Project Mogul, was launched on May 29, 1947.

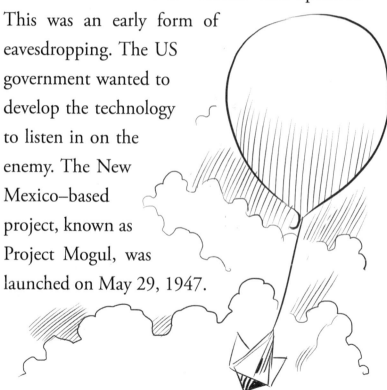

Project Mogul was top secret. Most people who worked on it did not even know it was called that! The team who worked at Alamogordo tested very high-flying balloons they hoped would be able to hear enemy bomb tests.

In June 1947, a weather balloon—launched by the Project Mogul team—crashed in the New Mexico desert. Summer thunderstorms and strange lightning patterns were common in the summer. But some Roswell residents weren't convinced the weather, or a weather balloon, had anything to do with the crash that night.

Was it a spy plane, or a flying saucer and its alien pilot?

The Term "Flying Saucer"

Before the crash at Roswell, alien spacecraft in science fiction books and movies were usually depicted as cylinders—a familiar rocket-like shape.

But on June 24, ten days after the crashed balloon was first spotted at Roswell, pilot Kenneth Arnold was flying his private plane in Washington State. He saw flashes of lights in the sky and nine large flat objects flying at very high speeds. He thought they could have been experimental military planes, but he wasn't sure. When Arnold described this sighting to a newspaper reporter, the objects were reported as being "flying saucers." Other observers claimed to have seen flying "pie plates" and "dimes." Two weeks later at Roswell, and forever after, the flattened disk shape was referred to as a "flying saucer."

CHAPTER 4
The Cold War Heats Up

After the end of World War II, and throughout the Cold War, people wondered if Russia could ever invade the United States. Could Communism spread that far? America raced to develop technology that would help make sure it didn't. And the US government worked hard to keep its intelligence secret. This fast-paced era of scientific development was leading both nations right into outer space.

At the start of the "space race," the Soviet Union was in the lead. It launched the very first artificial satellite into space on October 4, 1957. The satellite's low orbit made it visible all over the world with telescopes. It was called Sputnik 1, and the CIA wondered what it might lead to.

What else could the Russians launch? Spy cameras? Weapons? After Sputnik 1 was launched, the CIA feared that a Soviet satellite could now photograph any part of the world—including Area 51!

Sputnik 1

By the early 1960s, in addition to its own satellites, the United States had developed top secret spy planes called the U-2 and the A-12 Oxcart.

The U-2 was a spy plane that could carry up to seven hundred pounds of photographic equipment and spy on the Soviet Union by taking pictures from a very high altitude.

In the 1950s, a normal passenger plane flew just under twenty thousand feet above Earth. The A-12 could fly faster than a bullet at an altitude of ninety thousand feet!

After an American CIA pilot named Gary Powers was shot down by a Soviet missile in 1960, the United States knew that the secrets of their U-2 technology would be found out.

Francis Gary Powers was a second lieutenant jet pilot in the air force when he was recruited by the CIA in 1956. By 1960, he was well trained in carrying out secret missions in the air. His CIA U-2 spy plane was shot down while on a mission over the Soviet Union on May 1,

Francis Gary Powers

1960. He had been taking photographs at a very high altitude. When his plane crashed, it was damaged but not destroyed. The Soviets were able to recover its equipment and study the latest US-built technology of the plane.

Powers survived the crash, but he was convicted of espionage (spying) and sent to a Russian prison. After a year and nine months, he was exchanged in a "spy swap" for an American-held Soviet spy. His capture and the loss of his plane to enemy scientists is known as the U-2 Incident.

Powers stands trial in Moscow, Russia

After the U-2 Incident, the US government kicked their development of newer, and even faster, jets into high gear. And they used the CIA at Area 51 to do it.

These planes would fly faster and higher than had any aircraft before them. But the government didn't have the engineers and the factories to actually build the secret planes they had designed. So they gave contracts to private companies, like the American aerospace and technology company Lockheed Martin. Within Lockheed Martin, a division known as Skunk Works worked hard to build the new government-designed planes.

Skunk Works

The term *Skunk Works* is used by engineers to describe projects that are top secret. They may not even be officially listed in the company records. The Skunk Works division at Lockheed Martin is their secret development group in Palmdale, California.

In 1954, Skunk Works received their contract to build the U-2 spy plane. Nicknamed "Dragon Lady," the U-2 was the first jet that could fly as high as seventy thousand feet in all types of weather. By 1960, the original U-2 was being phased out. It was being replaced by the U-2C in 1960 and the U-2F in 1961.

As the difficult work of building their spy planes was carried out in Burbank, California, the CIA began enlarging their site at Area 51. They added a new five-thousand-foot runway on the lake bed, three new hangars, and better living quarters for the employees.

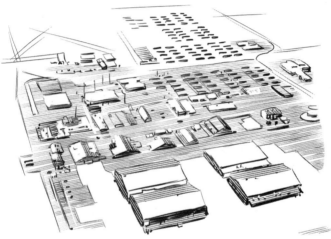

The very first A-12 was built at Lockheed's Skunk Works in 1962, and was driven to Area 51 on trailers marked "Wide Load." It took three days to move the well-disguised convoys from Burbank to Groom Lake. The CIA worked very hard to keep their testing secret.

They were experts in misinformation—leading people away from the truth. They called planes "articles" and pilots "drivers" in their reports. They used code names for everything. There was Project Oxcart as well as the air force's Project Have Doughnut, and Project Have Drill. Project Rainbow was the name given to a research project that worked to reduce the chances of the Soviets detecting U-2 planes.

Project Blue Book and Project Grudge were set up to record and study UFO sightings. And Project Saucer was established after pilot Arnold's sighting in Washington State. But UFO does not mean an alien aircraft. It's the term for any **u**nidentified **fl**ying **o**bject.

By 1962, Area 51 was no longer a temporary test site. It became a permanent US Air Force base. "No Trespassing" signs were placed around the outer edges of the property at this time.

Signs warned trespassers that they could be fined up to $1,000 and spend six months in jail! Photographs of the area were strictly forbidden.

Area 51 was now officially off-limits to anyone who didn't work there.

CHAPTER 5
UFOs or US Aircraft?

Throughout the early 1960s, test flights of the various U-2s, flying above seventy thousand feet, gave rise to a large number of strange sightings in the Nevada desert.

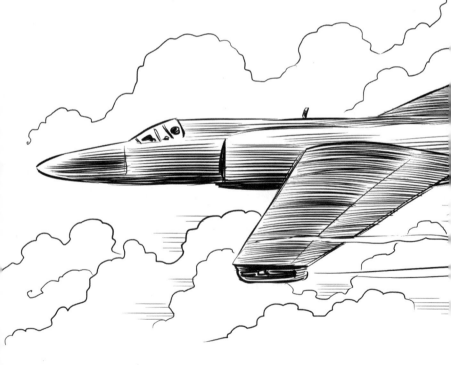

Although the official U-2 flight records can show dates that match the sightings, the public was not told this. They could not be made aware of the existence of any of the new aircraft that were in development at Area 51. The CIA's cover story—the one they told to the public and the press—was that they had special planes flying "weather observation missions."

When people saw strange colors in the sky and groups of lights seeming to fly in formation, they feared that the United States was being invaded by aliens.

Back in 1938, the alarming effects of broadcasting *The War of the Worlds,* a radio show, helped create not only a public fear of aliens, but also the need for the government to keep some of their programs top secret. They could not risk more public hysteria.

Although *The War of the Worlds* was only a play, the idea that Martians—or any type of alien

The New York Times.

Radio Listeners in Panic, Taking War Drama as Fact

Many Flee Homes to Escape 'Gas Raid From Mars'—Phone Calls Swamp Police at Broadcast of Wells Fantasy

or outsider—might invade at any moment stayed in the minds of the American people.

The War of the Worlds

Science fiction author H. G. Wells published *The War of the Worlds* in 1898. It tells the story of a Martian invasion of Earth. (*Martians* is the word used to describe aliens from Mars.)

Forty years later, in October 1938, the Mercury Theater broadcast a version of the story as a radio play. For over half an hour, dramatic "news bulletins" gave a horrific account of invaders from Mars landing in Grover's Mill, New Jersey. Although listeners were told in advance that the story was fiction, all across the country, people believed that the aliens and their war machines were headed to New York City.

Police stations and radio stations were overwhelmed by phone calls from frantic listeners. The narrator of the story, Orson Welles, later apologized for the realism of the broadcast and the terror it had created.

At the time, *The War of the Worlds* seemed to mirror tensions in Europe, where fears were brewing that Adolf Hitler of Germany was going to start a war.

Because the CIA remembered the public reaction to *The War of the Worlds*, they understood the value of keeping their test flights hidden from the public in the hills of Nevada at Area 51. But the test flights of the A-12 brought even more frequent sightings and speculation about the area. This was largely due to the fact that the new aircraft flew so much higher that to people on the ground, they looked elliptical (oval) in shape. By comparison, passenger planes flying much slower and at only twenty thousand feet were much easier to identify.

51

When people looked up at the Nevada night sky, they had no idea what the strange lights and flat, disk-like shapes could be. No one had ever seen planes that looked like that. So some people jumped to the conclusion that the UFOs were arriving from outer space.

Airline pilots even reported sightings to air traffic controllers on the ground and to the US Air Force! The CIA checked UFO sightings against the Project Oxcart flight logs of where and when the planes flew. The dates matched. But the public could not be let in on the secret.

By the end of the 1960s, five more hangars had been added to the Area 51 site, and the airspace above it was closed permanently. That meant that no planes—other than those taking off from or landing at the Groom Lake airfield—could fly over the area. The secrecy and security surrounding the region was even tighter than before. Because the test flights were frequent and the area was off-limits, people grew more alarmed that the government wouldn't explain the sightings. The fact that the US military denied anything was happening at the site just added to the mystery of Area 51.

CHAPTER 6
The Air Force Strikes Back

In the 1960s, the United States was fighting in South Vietnam, a small country on the South China Sea, to prevent a Communist takeover there.

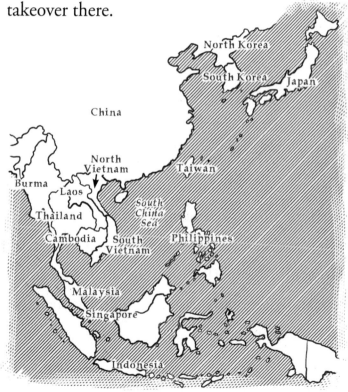

Southeast Asia in 1965

US Air Force planes were fighting against planes that had been built by the Soviets called MiGs. MiGs had been around since 1940, but the newest versions of this aircraft had never been seen before by US forces.

MiG-21F-13

The new MiG was the one plane that Americans did not know how to fight against and feared the most. The Soviet jet fighter didn't look at all like other Soviet planes. It had a sleek design that made it superfast and agile. It was able to turn and dive with ease. It could outmaneuver any American jet.

The US felt pressure to step up their quest for "an invisible plane" that could take on the MiG, because it wouldn't be detected on radar. In 1968, a Soviet-built MiG that had been captured by Israel was brought to Area 51. US engineers hoped to study the Soviet technology and test the Russian plane in secret at Groom Lake. They learned that US pilots would have to develop better flying skills and keep their planes at a higher speed in order to outmaneuver the MiG. But they were confident that with practice, they could do it! Pilots learned these skills at the newly formed Top Gun school.

Top Gun

The United States Navy Fighter Weapons School—nicknamed Top Gun—was established on March 3, 1969, just north of San Diego, California. At the former Naval Air Station Miramar, pilots learned how to outmaneuver enemy planes. The Top Gun school was invitation-only. That meant only the best and most capable pilots were trained there.

Throughout the early 1970s, US Navy pilots flew more successful missions against the Soviet MiG than the US Air Force, due to their training at Top Gun. The school is now known as the US Navy Strike Fighter Tactics Instructor Program.

While the team at Area 51 was busy studying the MiG fighter plane, the US Air Force had been collecting CIA reports on UFO sightings. Their mission—Project Blue Book—analyzed data to determine if UFOs were indeed real and a threat to the security of the country.

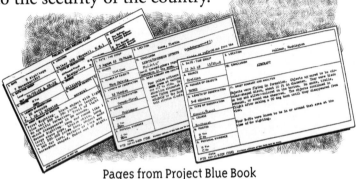

Pages from Project Blue Book

Project Blue Book had collected over twelve thousand UFO reports by 1969. They went over the reports and considered the following possibilities: Were the UFOs actually balloons, aircraft, meteors, stars or planets, searchlights, or natural occurrences such as cloud reflections and ice crystals? They also determined if UFO sightings were worthy of follow-up investigations.

Rules of Thumb

Ufologists—people interested in UFOs—consider many things in determining the believability of sightings.

1. Duration of sighting

2. Number of persons reporting the sighting

3. Location of sighting

4. Reliability of the person or persons giving the report

5. Number of individual sightings reported

6. Existence of physical evidence (photographs, material, hardware, etc.)

Project Blue Book determined that most UFO reports could be explained as natural occurrences or common aircraft. At the end of the study, it was concluded that nothing reported was a danger to national security, and that no evidence of any extraterrestrial vehicles had been found.

The US Air Force seemed happy with its UFO sightings task force. It just may have been the perfect project to keep the public distracted from the real work at Area 51.

CHAPTER 7
Conspiracies

The story of the Roswell crash had not been

Major Jesse Marcel

discussed for thirty years. Then it suddenly came to life again. It was revived by Major Jesse Marcel, who claimed to have been a witness to the aftermath of the crash. "I was there. It wasn't a balloon," he told the press and UFO researchers who were once again interested in the incident.

Other Roswell residents came forward and built on the original eyewitness accounts. Some claimed to have seen a spaceship or part of a disk.

Some said that small bodies with oversize heads, skinny arms, and large oval eyes had been seen in the shadows of the site. Arriving from the nearby army airfield, Steve Arnold claimed to have heard someone ask, "Are those *people*?!" about the four-foot-tall figures he claimed to have seen on the ground.

That same year, 1978, just as public interest in the site was growing, the US Air Force took full control of Area 51 from the CIA. But why? More and more people began to wonder if Area 51 actually *had* been storing and studying alien bodies that may have been sent from Roswell so long ago. They began traveling to the Nevada desert, curious to see what they might find.

Nowadays, one of the most popular ways to get close to Area 51 is by driving along the Extraterrestrial Highway.

The Extraterrestrial Highway

Since 1996, Nevada State Route 375 (Warm Springs Road) has also been known as the Extraterrestrial Highway. Many travelers have reported UFO sightings along this ninety-eight-mile stretch of road near Area 51. The small town of Rachel, Nevada, welcomes tourists and UFO hunters with alien-themed businesses such as the Little A'Le'Inn restaurant and motel.

Tourists hope that they might just spot a UFO or alien life-form while staying there, but most of the region surrounding the highway is uninhabited desert.

People are very interested in the land that surrounds the actual restricted area around Groom Lake. The city of Las Vegas is about seventy-five miles away. Janet Airlines, which may stand for Joint Air Network for Employee Transportation, flies out of McCarran Airport to Area 51 daily. But this airline is not for tourists. This is the private commuter fleet of six planes for Area 51. It was established in 1972 to ferry employees on and off the base, and can carry up to 1,200 people a day!

As expected, plenty of mystery surrounds the airline known locally as "UFO Airlines." The flight attendants must have top secret security clearance from the air force before they are hired. The window shades are often kept closed so that passengers cannot look down onto Area 51—even though they are traveling to work there.

As the public became more aware of the existence of Area 51, they wondered what might be happening in such a secretive place on the desert valley floor surrounded by mountains. They began to imagine that there might be a conspiracy—a secret plan—in place at Area 51. But a plan to do what?

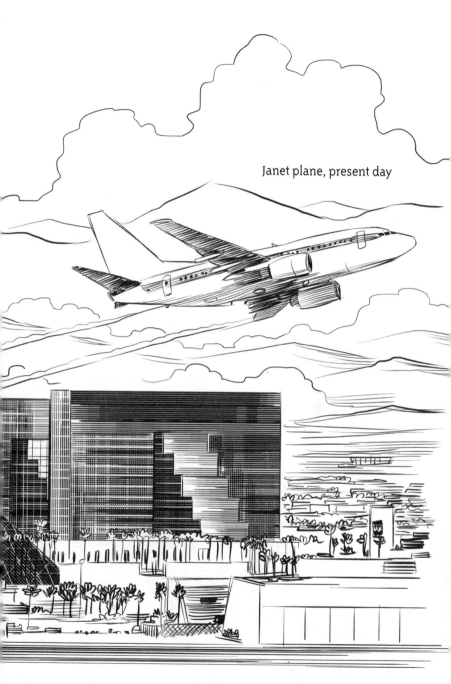

Janet plane, present day

CHAPTER 8
The Box

The US government provides very little information about Area 51. It is permanently off-limits, which means they plan to *never* allow access to the site. Security clearance for employees is checked regularly. There are buried motion sensors everywhere on the property. And no one ever even thinks about bringing a camera to work.

But in April 1974, photos of Area 51 did appear. They were taken by astronauts on board Skylab, even though the CIA had specifically given "instructions not to do this." (The airfield at Groom Lake was the only location in the world that had such instructions.)

Skylab

Operating from 1973 to 1979, Skylab was the first US space station to orbit Earth. The NASA-launched station housed a workshop, living quarters, and a solar observatory. It was equipped with everything necessary to sustain the crew: food, water, medicine, supplies, and breathable air. Skylab functioned as an orbiting laboratory. The scientific experiments that took place on Skylab included photographing Earth and observing the sun in new and important ways.

Although previous US and Soviet crews had spent up to eighteen days on space missions, the Skylab crew would spend up to eighty-four days orbiting Earth!

When Skylab was launched, Area 51 didn't even—officially—exist. The CIA and the US Air Force had never acknowledged their base there. They made no mention of it by name. Pilots who flew there and in the surrounding airspace had only ever referred to the area as "the box."

All that the Skylab photos showed was long-range aerial shots of Area 51. Nothing to make headlines. Truly shocking news didn't break until a few years later, in 1978, when former employees of Area 51 came forth, claiming they had seen—and worked with—aliens, or parts of alien ships.

Aerial view of Area 51

Their statements helped create many myths and new conspiracy theories involving the research and work conducted at Area 51.

Then, in 1989, a former Area 51 security guard, Bob Lazar, said he was breaking the oath of secrecy to speak about his work publicly. He claimed that there were nine alien spacecraft at Area 51, and that he had actually seen an alien body at the site!

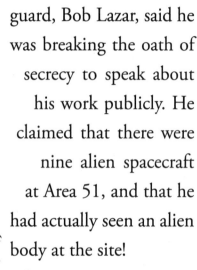

Bob Lazar

Lazar gave an interview to a Las Vegas television station that was eventually broadcast in Japan, and then around the world. He said that he saw "proof from another planet, another system, another intelligence."

Lazar's statements only added to the conspiracy theories that were prompted by the secrecy at Groom Lake. The government denied that Bob Lazar ever worked for them.

The public's curiosity about this off-limits area reached peak levels in the early 1990s. Why wouldn't the government comment on work that was being done there?

In 1994, the US government released its final word on Roswell in a press statement. They wanted people to know that they had looked for evidence of an alien crash. The statement said that the wreckage in Roswell had been a nuclear-test spy balloon from Project Mogul. And a 1997 report said that the bodies, which were not found at the Roswell crash but in later incidents, were simply crash-test dummies used to test high-altitude parachutes. But many people did not believe the reports. They believed the government was still hiding the truth.

One of the most popular ideas to emerge is the theory that *something* from beyond our solar system was captured that night in Roswell back in 1947, and that scientists have been studying the components of it ever since. People even believe that alien materials have led to our own development of now common things like Kevlar fiber (used to make bulletproof vests), and have greatly contributed to our manned space flights and satellite systems.

When we study the parts of something to investigate how it was made in order to make something similar or to re-create it, we call it reverse engineering. This might include taking something apart to analyze the design details, its electrical components, its chemical makeup, and any computer programs.

When Neil Armstrong spoke to mission control from the moon in 1969, he used an early type of cell phone that was developed by the Motorola company. Was the "phone" reverse engineered from alien communications technology that came from Area 51? Could there have been a group of Skunk Works scientists at

Motorola? Conspiracy theorists believe this is one of the best examples of reverse engineering.

Some people believe that we have reverse engineered other things such as NASA spacecraft, computers, and lasers from alien technology stored and studied at Area 51.

CHAPTER 9
Is There an Area 52?

In 2013, many Area 51 documents were declassified. That meant that the CIA no longer considered them to be a secret.

There are some people who believe that the air force base is exactly what it claims to be: a US government site where new flight technology is developed. They think the *real* secrets may be kept in another location altogether.

Where might it be?

The Dugway Proving Ground in the Utah desert is one guess. It is a US Army facility that was established in 1942 to test chemical and biological weapons—weapons that could transmit new kinds of poison. The property covers more than 1,200 square miles of the Great Salt Lake Desert. It is larger than the state of Rhode Island and is the largest "special-use" airspace in the United States.

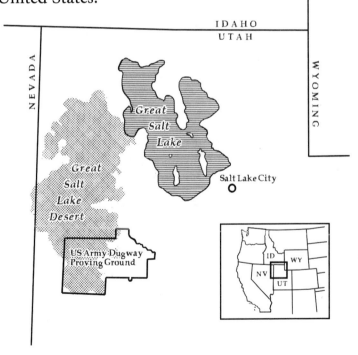

Dugway has been used as an army training ground to teach soldiers about desert survival. It is also the home of several radar tracking systems. It is sometimes referred to as "Area 52" because of the great secrecy that surrounds it. The area's closely guarded secrets first came to national attention in 1968, when thousands of sheep on neighboring ranches died almost overnight.

The Dugway Sheep Incident

On March 17, 1968, thousands of sheep were mysteriously found dead by ranchers in the area of Skull Valley, about twenty-seven miles from the Dugway Proving Ground in Utah. Over the next several days, the total number climbed to over six thousand. They had been grazing in the afternoon and were dead by the next morning. It was later proven that the sheep had been poisoned by chemical testing at the army base at Dugway.

This incident contributed to the growing suspicions that the government was testing more than airplanes in its large open spaces in the US desert. The Dugway Proving Ground was manufacturing some very unsafe chemicals. Armies can use the chemicals as weapons when they put them inside bombs or shoot them from guns. They cause irritation, injury, and even death. This led to a public outcry against the use of deadly chemical weapons by the US Army.

It also created a lot of speculation—new theories formed without much evidence—about what *else* might be going on at Dugway. Once people learned about the chemical testing, they wondered what other secrets might be kept there.

There is even talk that the Dugway Proving Ground could actually be a military spaceport for alien craft—a sort of landing and launching pad for extraterrestrials. But if that could possibly be true, where are all the aliens? Most astronomers think there will never be an alien invasion. However, an Italian physicist named Enrico Fermi made a pretty good case for believing in the possibility.

Enrico Fermi

The Fermi Paradox

A paradox is when two statements that seem to contradict each other are both probably true. Fermi pointed out that our sun is a common type of star. It has planets orbiting it, one of which—Earth—has life on it. With millions of other similar stars in the universe, the odds must be strong that intelligent life has evolved in other solar systems. If true, then some of those intelligent beings should have mastered space travel by now, and Earth would have been visited by aliens a long time ago. However, there is no evidence—no sign at all—that alien life has contacted us or visited Earth. Fermi's simple question was "Where is everybody?" If space travel is possible, then where are the aliens? This is known as the Fermi Paradox. Fermi created the world's first nuclear reactor. And he won the Nobel Prize for physics in 1938.

The first nuclear reactor

Some people suspect that the US government is content to have people constantly guessing about the activities at Area 51. Because about four hundred miles away, in the Utah desert, they are keeping even bigger secrets at the place that has come to be thought of as Area 52.

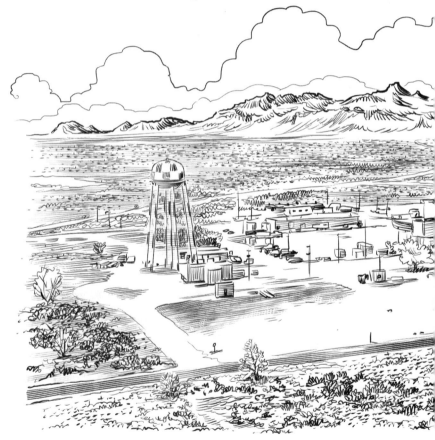

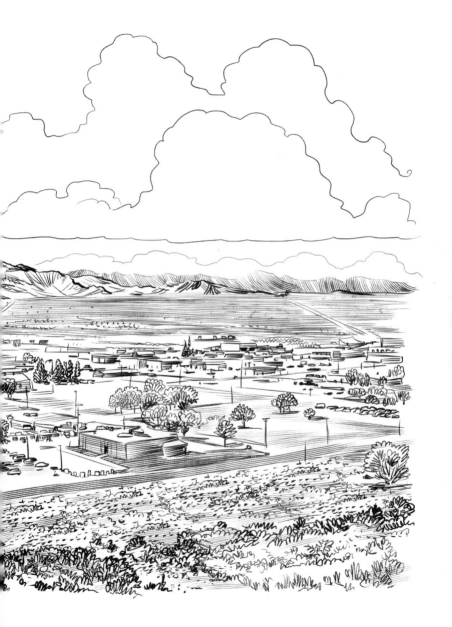

CHAPTER 10
Area 51 Today

There are no fences around Area 51, only orange posts, signs, and plenty of surveillance cameras. Any approaching vehicle is detected by electronic sensors that let the military security know where it is and how fast it's traveling. Guards are allowed to shoot anyone who approaches the site on foot.

Although the 2013 documents declassify Area 51 as an "official entity," it still remains top secret. Many in the US government believe the need for such a secret space is now greater than ever. A 2010 article in Smithsonian's *Air & Space* magazine reported that $30 to $36 billion a year is spent developing new technologies at Area 51, much of it on the classified or "black" world of secret military projects and programs. That's nearly $100 million *a day*!

The creators of the first atomic bomb wrote the rules for black ops. But Area 51 was the first "black facility" in US history. It operates completely outside the US federal budget and without budget oversight from the federal government. The laws of the US government do not apply to what happens at Area 51. Some people think this is the most dangerous kind of secret to have.

Black Ops

A black operation (black op, for short) is a secret mission by a government or the military. A black op usually has a double layer of security: Beyond being secret, the black op usually cannot be traced to the person or group who is in charge of it.

If there has been a deliberate attempt to cover up the real group or person behind the black op and put the blame on someone else, that kind of deception is known as a "false flag."

A "black budget" is money set aside for the most top secret projects (often black ops). A black budget is hidden from the public, government employees, and sometimes even the Congress of the United States.

Area 51 continues to operate as the testing ground facility for stealth technology that is both manned (by trained air force pilots) and unmanned, including rockets, satellites, and surface-to-air missiles without humans on board. These are projects that we will not learn about for years to come.

The people who create and maintain black ops are very good at what they do. They have been protecting their work for a very long time.

Even though the Cold War ended in 1991, the military continues to develop sophisticated robotic aircraft, including unmanned aerial vehicles (UAVs), commonly known as drones. In 2002, the first combat missile was fired from a UAV. These pilotless craft can look for enemies in areas that are too dangerous for soldiers to venture into. They make it possible to fight wars without putting troops in danger. Because it remains such a remote secret, Area 51 is still a great location to test such missiles.

The sixtieth anniversary of the U-2 program was celebrated in August 2015. Lockheed Martin's Skunk Works announced that they were developing the next generation of the U-2, called the TR-X. In 2016, they confirmed that the TR-X would be unmanned and fly up to seventy thousand feet above the earth.

Since the height of the Cold War in the 1950s and 1960s, the CIA has confirmed that over half of all UFO sightings were caused by test flights of American spy planes. Because the shape of the A-12 planes was wide and flat with bright silver exteriors, they looked unlike any plane before them. They were impossible for anyone on the ground to identify. Once A-12 planes began flying, UFO sightings increased dramatically.

Even after such admissions, the public will probably only ever know what the CIA wants us to know about their research and testing at Area 51. The agency's number one most-read tweet on their "Best of 2014 List" was: "Reports of unusual activity in the skies in the '50s? It was us." And it only took them sixty years to admit it.

But by the time that tweet was sent, most Americans had already accepted the idea that Area 51 was a strange place that just *might* be the home of all things otherworldly.

Indiana Jones and Hangar 51

The mysterious warehouse seen at the end of *Raiders of the Lost Ark* is a fictional US military base where thousands of secret items are stored. Although the Ark of the Covenant is eventually brought there, it's not until the fourth movie in the Indiana Jones series, *Indiana Jones and the Kingdom of the Crystal Skull*, that we learn the location's true name: Hangar 51.

Like the real-life Area 51, it is hidden deep in the Nevada desert and considered top secret. In addition to the Ark, thirteen alien bodies, called "interdimensional beings," are stored in wooden crates there.

By 2008, when *Kingdom of the Crystal Skull* opened, using the number "51" had come to indicate something secret—and perhaps out of this world.

For decades, people feared the secrets that might be kept at Area 51. But then movies like *Indiana Jones and the Kingdom of the Crystal Skull* and television shows  like *The X-Files*, and even *The Simpsons* made Area 51 seem like one of the coolest places on Earth.

We don't know for sure what is happening at Area 51. What we *do* know for certain is that aircraft designed by air force engineers and manufactured by human hands fly there all the time. The airspace is used to test things the public most often cannot know about.

The closest any of us will ever get to "knowing" is a mountain in Lincoln County, Nevada, called Tikaboo Peak. It is twenty-six miles east of Area 51 and the closest point with a perfectly legal view of the area.

The secrecy of the government's operations, the speculation about flying saucers and alien invaders, and the lure of mysterious historical events in this part of the American desert will probably always draw people to Area 51. But it might be wise to go no farther than Tikaboo Peak.

Timeline of Area 51

1947 — Project Mogul is launched in the New Mexico desert on May 29

— The remains of a weather balloon are found in Roswell, New Mexico, on June 14

1954 — Lockheed Martin's Skunk Works receives a contract to build the first U-2 spy plane

1955 — The land surrounding Groom Lake, Nevada, including former silver mines, is acquired by the US Air Force from the Atomic Energy Commission for use as a CIA test site

1960 — Gary Powers's U-2 spy plane is shot down over Soviet Russia

1962 — Area 51 becomes a permanent US Air Force base

1968 — Thousands of sheep are found dead around Skull Valley, Utah, near the Dugway Proving Ground

— Project Blue Book reports conclude that there is no threat to US national security from UFOs

1978 — The US Air Force takes full control of Area 51 from the CIA

1989 — Bob Lazar claims to have seen alien bodies and spacecraft while working at Area 51

1994 — The US government releases its final word on Roswell, saying that it was, in fact, a surveillance balloon from Project Mogul

1998 — The US Air Force admits that the facility at Area 51 exists

2013 — The CIA formally acknowledges the existence of their base at Area 51, and makes many documents public

Timeline of the World

1947 — Mahatma Gandhi begins his march for peace in East Bengal, India, on January 2

1950 — Chuck Cooper is drafted as the first black player in the NBA

— Uruguay defeats Brazil 2–1 in soccer's fourth World Cup

1955 — The first nuclear submarine, USS *Nautilus*, begins its first voyage

1962 — Jamaica gains independence from Great Britain

— The Beatles sign their first recording contract with EMI Parlophone

1968 — Vietnam peace talks begin in Paris between the United States and North Vietnam, but the war doesn't end until 1975

1972 — The first two female FBI agents begin their training

1978 — The Bee Gees' album *Saturday Night Fever* is number one for twenty-four weeks

1984 — Apple Computer, Inc. debuts the Macintosh personal computer

1989 — Germans begin demolishing the Berlin Wall on November 10

1991 — The Soviet Union collapses

1994 — Nelson Mandela becomes South Africa's first black president

1999 — NASA launches the Mars Polar Lander

2017 — Scientists in Central China find the fossil remains of the oldest known human ancestor—450-million-year-old *Saccorhytus*

Bibliography

*Books for young readers

*Aguilar, David A. *Cosmic Catastrophes.* New York: Viking/
 Penguin Random House LLC, 2016.

Corso, Colonel Philip J. *The Day After Roswell.* New York: Pocket
 Books/Simon & Schuster, 1997.

Jacobsen, Annie. *Area 51: An Uncensored History of America's
 Top Secret Military Base.* New York: Little Brown and
 Company, 2011.

*Krasner, Barbara. *The Mystery of Area 51.* Minneapolis: Abdo
 Publishing, 2016.

*Martin, Ted. *Area 51.* The Unexplained. Minneapolis: Bellwether
 Media, 2012.

Meltzer, Brad, with Keith Ferrell. *History Decoded: The 10
 Greatest Conspiracies of All Time.* New York: Workman
 Publishing Co., 2013.

Merlin, Peter W. *Images of Aviation: Area 51.* Charleston: Arcadia
 Publishing, 2011.

Nelson, Paul. *Area 51: The CIA's Secret Files.* Aired October 12, 2014,
 on National Geographic Channel. natgeotv.com/asia/area-51-
 the-cias-secret-files.

Steiger, Brad. *Project Blue Book.* New York: Ballantine Books/
 Random House, 1976.

Story, David. *UFO Hunters.* **Season 3, episode 13, "Area 52."** Aired
 October 29, 2009 on History Channel.